YOUR KNOWLEDGE HAS VALUE

AF144145

- We will publish your bachelor's and master's thesis, essays and papers

- Your own eBook and book - sold worldwide in all relevant shops

- Earn money with each sale

Upload your text at www.GRIN.com
and publish for free

Corinna Schmidt

The effects of a cut in interest rates on the current UK economy as a whole and on EaszJet plc.

GRIN Publishing

Bibliographic information published by the German National Library:

The German National Library lists this publication in the National Bibliography;
detailed bibliographic data are available on the Internet at http://dnb.dnb.de .

Imprint:

Copyright © 2009 GRIN Verlag GmbH
Print and binding: Books on Demand GmbH, Norderstedt Germany
ISBN: 978-3-656-87403-4

This book at GRIN:

http://www.grin.com/en/e-book/127763/the-effects-of-a-cut-in-interest-rates-on-
the-current-uk-economy-as-a-whole

GRIN - Your knowledge has value

Since its foundation in 1998, GRIN has specialized in publishing academic texts by students, college teachers and other academics as e-book and printed book. The website www.grin.com is an ideal platform for presenting term papers, final papers, scientific essays, dissertations and specialist books.

Visit us on the internet:

http://www.grin.com/

http://www.facebook.com/grincom

http://www.twitter.com/grin_com

Introduction

The UK economy is facing a significant downturn. After the V.A.T. reduction failed the expected increase in consumer spending, the UK uses intermediaries of the Monetary Policy (MP) to stimulate the economy. On the March, 5th 2009, the Bank of England announced that they lower the bank rate paid to commercial banks from 1% to 0,5% to ensure that the inflation target of 2 % will be achieved. (www.bankofengland.co.uk) On the base of the economic theory it will be discussed what the influences of a cut in interest rates are on the UK economy, the effects on the current financial situation and on easyJet plc.

Explain using economic theory what the effects of a cut in interest rates will be on the UK economy as a whole.

The Bank of England's Monetary Policy Committee (MPC) is responsible for the stability in the financial system. One of their functions is to change the interest rate to adjust the inflation to forecasted developments in the Consumer Price Index (CPI). (Sloman 2007 p. 284) A cut in the rate of interest affects the macro-economy because it increases the money supply and simulates the aggregate demand (AD). This is known as transmission mechanism (Sloman 2007 p. 296) and affects the economic cycle in different ways.

BoE lends money to financial institutions, such as commercial banks and building societies. If the banks borrow money for a lower interest rate, they match their interest rates for their customers.

Firstly, a reduced interest rate makes saving less interesting for consumers. This is because savings accounts don't achieve high profits anymore. Instead consumers tend to lend and spend more money. (www.bankofengland.co.uk) And a higher consumption of domestically produced goods and services leads to a higher output of production. (Sloman, 2007 p. 238) If companies produce more the demand for labour rises what brings down unemployment. This is called accommodation. (Anderton 2006 p.602)

Secondly, the interest rate is an important determinant of investment. A fall in the market rate makes investments more profitable for companies because the expected return on investment rises. (Hardwick et al. 1999 p. 422)

1

Thirdly, higher spending increases the velocity of money and the cash flow of companies. This makes companies more confident that sales figures will rise and they increase their production and are encouraged to invest more. (Sloman 2007 p. 301)

Fourthly, it also increases the price of assets, such as shares, bonds and house prices. But the interest payments due on loans and mortgage rates decreases. (www.bankofengland.co.uk)

Additionally, a reduction of the interest rate influences the exchange rate. If the interest rate is lowered the exchange rate for Sterling falls, because of decreasing demand. (Anderton 2006 p. 569) This makes the UK more competitive in the global market. When the Sterling is worth less, foreign countries tend to import more goods from the UK. A higher net-external demand increases the production of UK companies. However, the import of goods slows down, because foreign currencies become more expensive what makes import less attractive. (Sloman 2007, p. 297)

Overall, those factors are stimulating the AD and bring the national output in the UK closer to its productive potential. (Sloman 2007 p. 267) Because, a rise in consumer and government consumption, an increase in the level of investment and export, followed by a slowdown in import, leads to a macroeconomic equilibrium. That means a rise in the GDP and a growth in national wealth. (Sloman 2007 p. 267)

Graph 1

Figure 1: From interest rates to inflation – the transmission mechanism of monetary policy

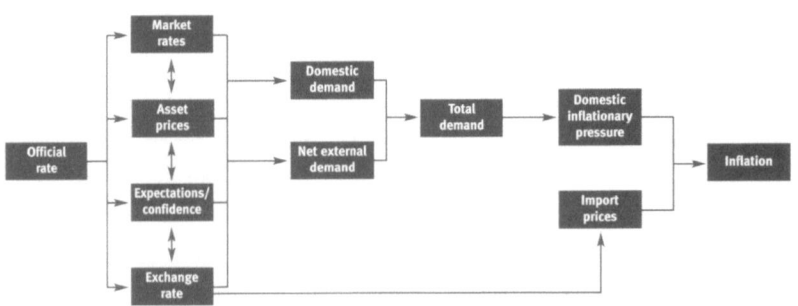

(Source:www.Bankofengland.co.uk)

2

The UK economy is currently experiencing a downward trend caused by broken sub-prime mortgage deals in the US. House prices have fallen dramatically. Consumer confidence changed negatively what lowered the demand for goods in the last year. This led the UK into recession and will cause the CPI to fall under the 2% target in the medium term. (The Sunday Times, Smith)

To weaken the negative effects of the financial crisis and to escape a deflation, the UK increases the money supply. The operation on the open market is carried out with quantitative easing of £75bn over the next quarter and the reduction of the interest rate.(www.bankofengland.co.uk) Those intermediaries of the MP are determined to stimulate investors and consumers to spend more money. The rise in spending causes inflation(see graph 1). It erodes the value of money and raises price levels without a rise in real income. (Anderton, 2006 p. 600) The inflation ensures that the 2% target will be reached and a deflation will be avoided. This are urgent steps for the economy, but the danger is that if money supply exceeds demand it drives inflation to high and reduces the wealth status dramatically. (www.timesonline.co.uk)

Other issues of this government approach could be emerged by financial institutions. Some commercial banks, such as RBS, have been hit hard by the credit crisis and needed to become partly nationalised. Rising concerns are that banks will hoard the extra cash instead lending it to investors on the lower rate. (The Sunday Times, Smith)
In a recession consumers are unconfident about the financial system, therefore they tend to save their money instead of spending it. Or consumers invest in more risky funds because they promise higher revenues. (The Sunday Times, Smith) That would lead to an excess of money supply. With no spending made by consumers, firms need to cut down on production because of decreasing demand.

Real implications of a cut in interest rates can't be measured in advanced because changes do not occur instantaneously. The influences of the change in interest rate will appear in the medium term and affect the economic system after 18 months. (Anderton 2006 p. 570). Furthermore, the UK is currently using several monetary and fiscal intermediaries. All those components are directly linked to each other and therefore the real effect on the future UK economy is uncertain.

What would be the impact on large blue-chip companies? - easyJet plc

In the last 6 months it could be noticed that flight passengers are trading down to low-cost airlines, such as easyJet plc. easyJet`s positive revenue affirms that. The revenue in the final months of 2008 grew higher than forecasted by 32% to £550m. (www.easyJet.com-Statement) The change of the interest rates will contribute this rise in easyJet passenger numbers. It enables more customers to afford a short vacation on credit.

Besides rising revenues, easyJet`s net income decreased as a result of rising cost of goods sold as a percentage of sales from 57.27% to 64.07%.(www.ft.com/marketsdata) easyJet needed to increase capital expenditure to mitigate the negative impacts of the financial crisis. The Dept on total capital ratio increased to 0,55%. The return on investment fell to just 4.08%. The current ratio of 1.56:1 demonstrates a lack in liquidity. In fact easyJet`s cash reserves fell by £86.90m. (www.ft.com/marketsdata)

Therefore, lower interest rates enables easyJet plc to acquire a higher liquidity for new investments. Full-service airlines cut down their capacity because of shrinking demand.(www.ft.com/marketsdata) easyJet could win those market shares by increasing capacities and investing into its main European bases. Also it allows investment for launching new routes and expanding the aircraft fleet. Furthermore, it will provide a better cash flow for easyJet to survive extra expenditures such as raising fuel costs what can be caused by fluctuating dollar rates. (easyJet.com)

A negative effect of reduced interest rates could be the depreciating Sterling. Due to that fact that 51% of easyJet's revenue is drawn in the EURO-currency zone (wwweasyJet.com-presentation), a stronger EURO could have an adverse effect on the revenue.

Graph 2

EASYJET EZJ:LSE PERFORMANCE FROM OCTOBER 2008 – FEBRUARY 2009

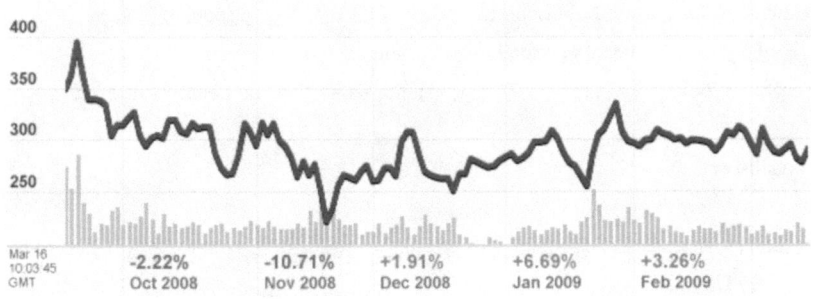

	-2.22%	-10.71%	+1.91%	+6.69%	+3.26%
Mar 16 10:03:45 GMT	Oct 2008	Nov 2008	Dec 2008	Jan 2009	Feb 2009

(source: www.FT.com)

Conclusion

A cut in interest rates has a wide impact on the UK economy. It increases the demand for money and stimulates investors and consumers to spend more. Additionally, it influences the exchange rate for the Sterling. The AD for internal goods rises and encourages firms to produce more. This brings the aggregate supply and demand closer to the micro economic equilibrium. But in times of recession, the expected effects of higher money supply are not necessarily reached.

Low-cost airline easyJet plc is a winner of the economic downturn. Because customers are trading down to value flights, easyJet expands its market share. Increasing costs for easyJet lowered its liquidity and the net income decreased. But, low interest rates helps easyJet plc to gain liquidity to survive potential high losses as consequences of the recession.

(Total word count: 1.362)

5

Bibliography

Anderton, A. (2006) (4th ed.) Economics Essex: Pearson Education Limited

Hardwick, P. Langmead, J. Bahadur, K. (1999) (5th ed.) An Introduction to Modern
   Economics London: Pearson Education Limited

Sloman, J. (2007) (4th ed.) Essentials of Economics Essex: Pearson Education Limited

Newspapers

The Sunday Times/Business – Bank injection means we are all monetarists now (08.03.2009)
   By David Smith

Internet resources:

Bank of England – How the Monetary Policy works
   http://www.bankofengland.co.uk/monetarypolicy/how.htm
   (accessed 11.03.2009)

Bank of England - Publications
   http://www.bankofengland.co.uk/publications/news/2009/019.htm
   (accessed 11.03.2009)

EasyJet – Interim analysis presentation
   http://www.easyjet.com/common/img/q1_2009_interim_analyst_presentation.pdf
   (accessed 13.03.2009)

EasyJet – First quarter interim Management Statement
   http://www.easyjet.com/common/img/q1_2009_trading_statement.pdf
   (accessed 13.03.2009)

Financial Times Online – easyJet plc Summary
   http://markets.ft.com/tearsheets/financialsSummary.asp?symbol=UK:EZJ
   (accessed 13.03.2009)

The Times Online – What is quantitative easing? How it works? (05.03.2009)
   Author not stated
   http://business.timesonline.co.uk/tol/business/economics/article5850466.ece
   (accessed 14.03.2009)